THE ESSENTIAL COLLECTION

BEETHOVEN

GOLD

Published by
Chester Music Limited
14-15 Berners Street, London W1T 3LJ, UK.

Exclusive Distributors:
Music Sales Limited
Distribution Centre, Newmarket Road, Bury St Edmunds, Suffolk IP33 3YB, UK.
Music Sales Corporation
180 Madison Avenue, 24th Floor, New York NY 10016, USA.
Music Sales Pty Limited
4th floor, Lisgar House, 30-32 Carrington Street, Sydney, NSW 2000, Australia.
Order No. CH80135
ISBN 978-1-78038-747-5
This book © Copyright 2012 by Chester Music.

Symphonies 3,5,6,7,9, Piano Concerto No.5 and the Violin Concerto arranged by Jack Long.
Music engraved by Note-orious Productions Limited.
CD Project Manager: Ruth Power.
CD recorded and produced by Mutual Chord Studio, Guangzhou, China.
Previously published as Book Only Edition CH65670.

Book printed and CD manufactured in the EU.

Your Guarantee of Quality:
As publishers, we strive to produce every book to the highest commercial standards.
The music has been carefully designed to minimise awkward page turns
and to make playing from it a real pleasure.
Particular care has been given to specifying acid-free, neutral-sized
paper made from pulps which have not been elemental chlorine bleached.
This pulp is from farmed sustainable forests and was produced
with special regard for the environment.
Throughout, the printing and binding have been planned to ensure a sturdy,
attractive publication which should give years of enjoyment.
If your copy fails to meet our high standards, please inform us and we will gladly replace it.

www.musicsales.com

CHESTER MUSIC
part of The Music Sales Group

London / New York / Paris / Sydney / Copenhagen / Berlin / Madrid / Hong Kong / Tokyo

Sonatina in G major

Composed by Ludwig van Beethoven

Moderato

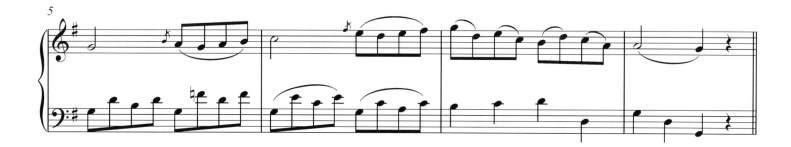

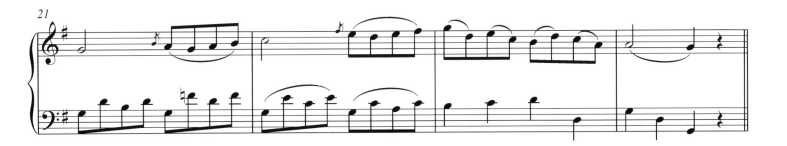

5

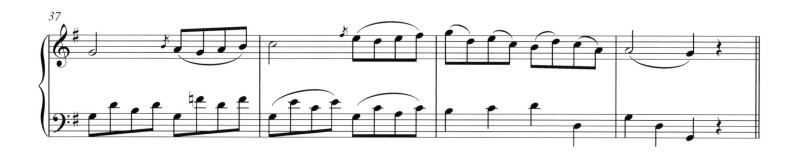

Für Elise

Composed by Ludwig van Beethoven

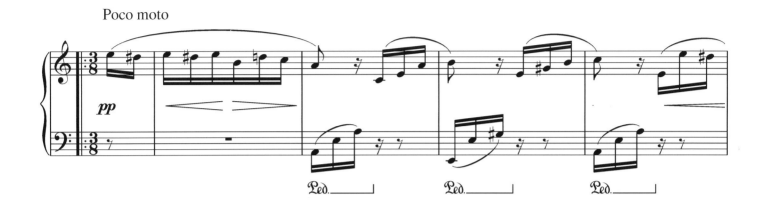

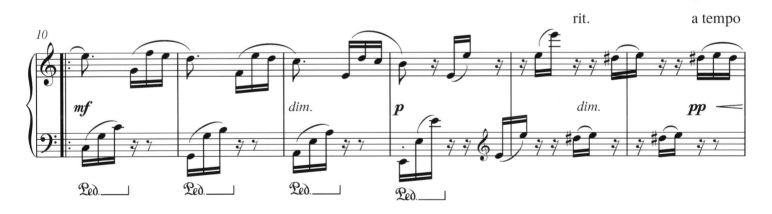

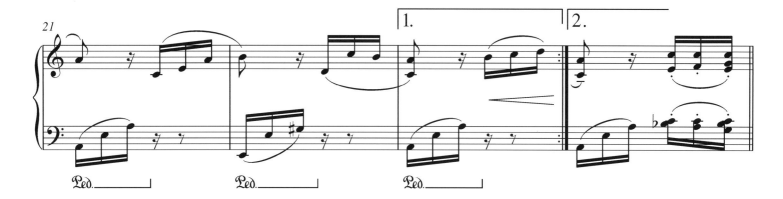

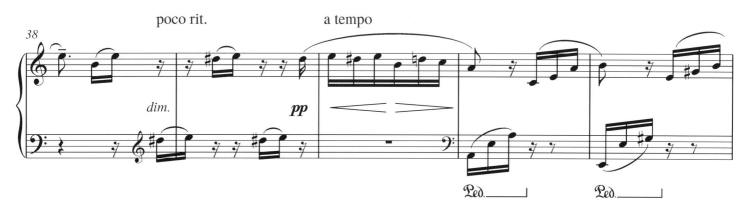

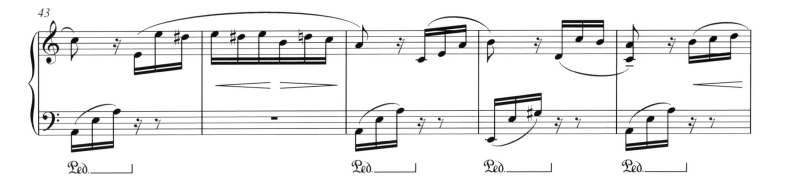

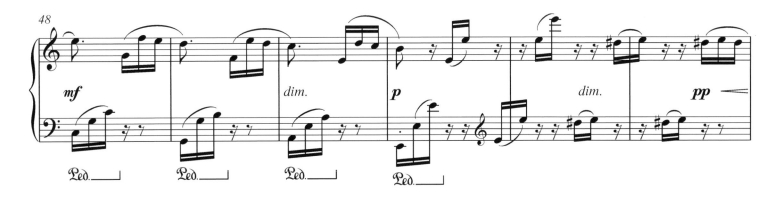

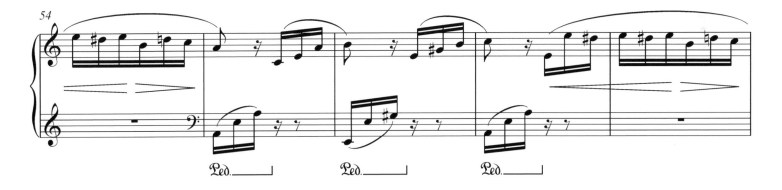

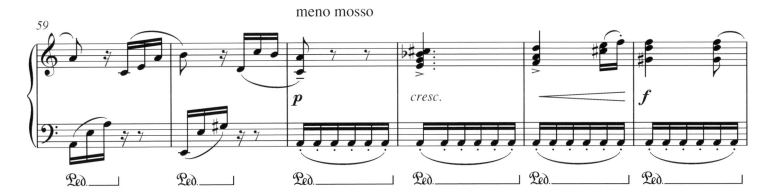

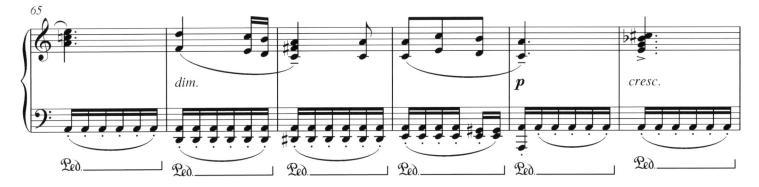

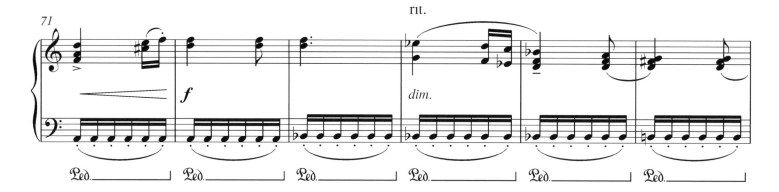

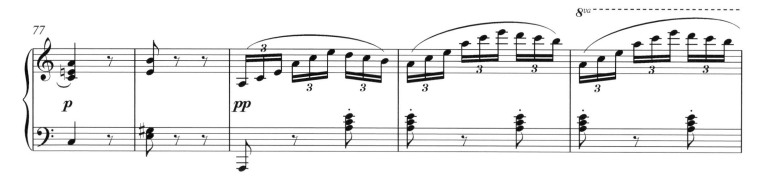

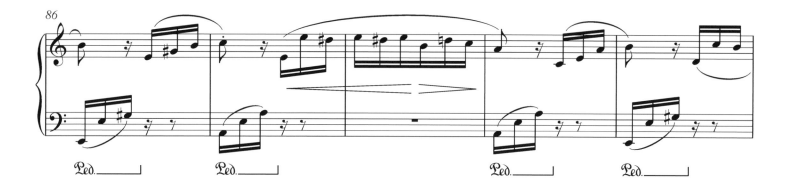

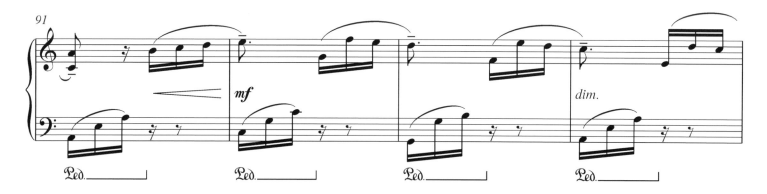

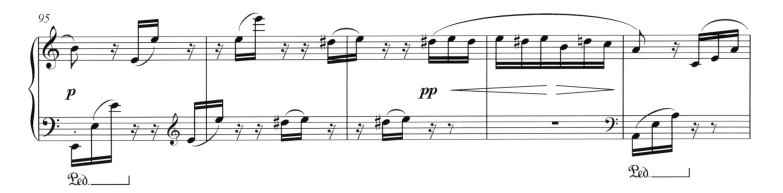

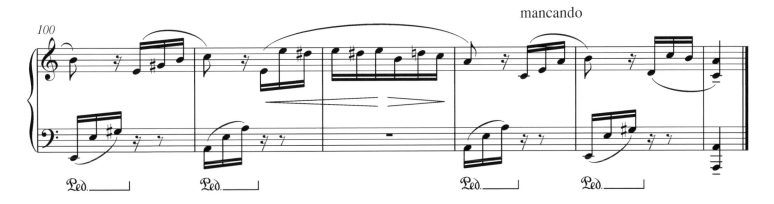

Minuet in G major
(WoO 10)

Composed by Ludwig van Beethoven

Allegretto (♩ = 120)

Fine

TRIO

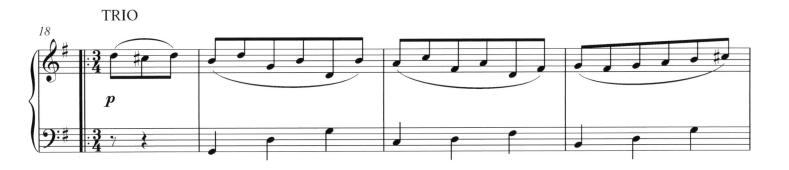

Minuet da capo

Rondo in A major
(WoO 49)

Composed by Ludwig van Beethoven

Allegretto

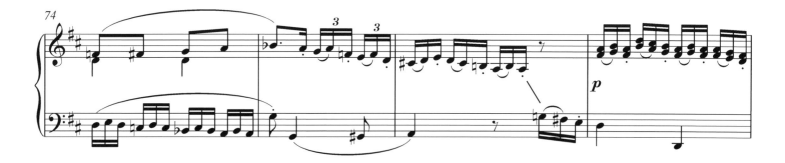

Moonlight Sonata Op. 27, No. 2
(Sonata quasi una Fantasia)

Composed by Ludwig van Beethoven

Adagio sostenuto

sempre **pp**

una corda

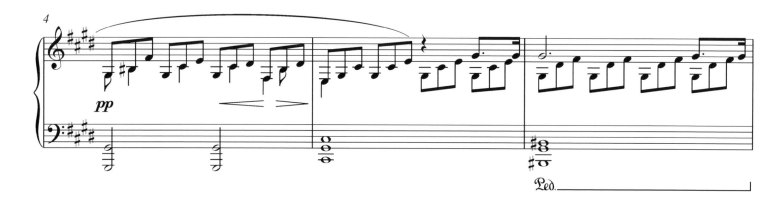

pp

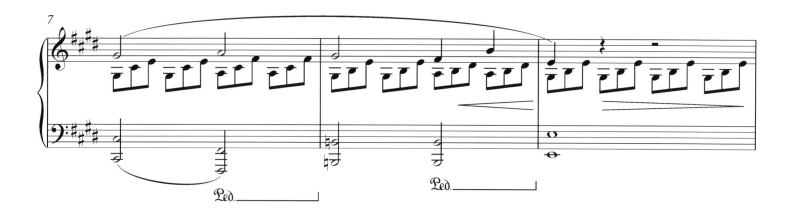

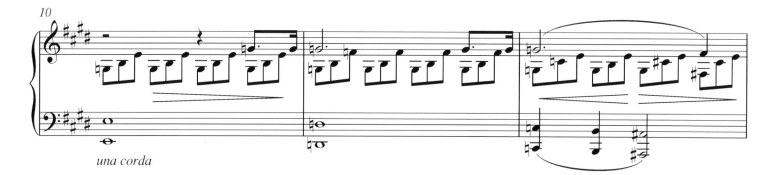

una corda

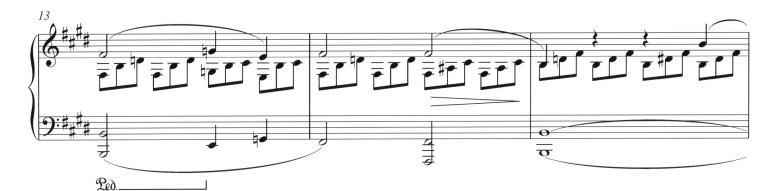

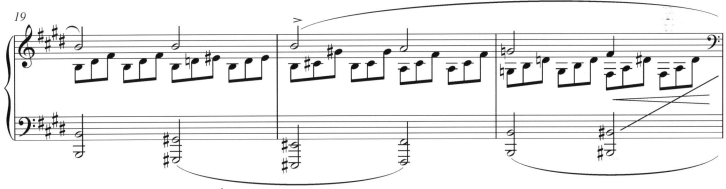

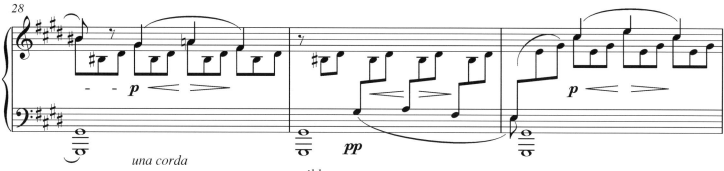

una corda

il basso sempre

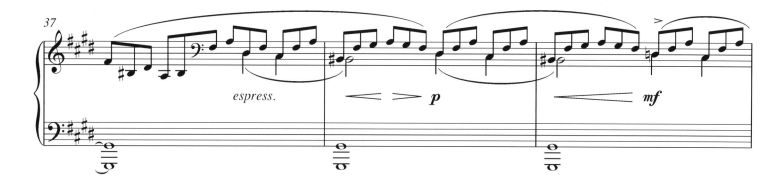

poco rit.   a tempo   più marcato del principio

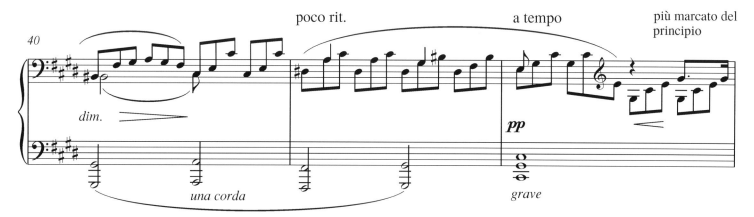

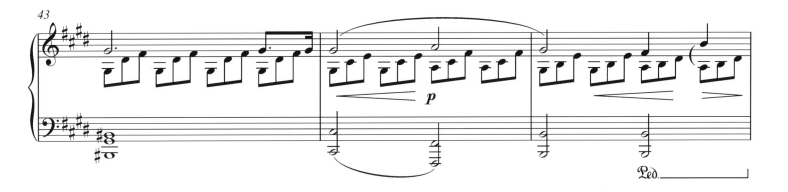

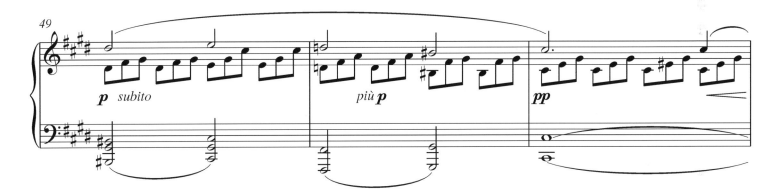

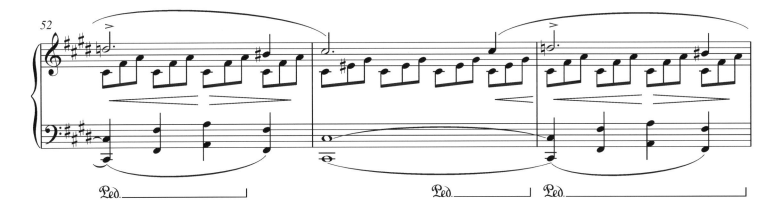

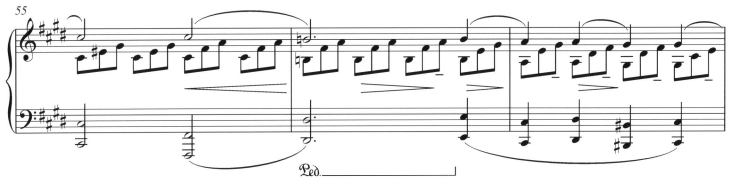

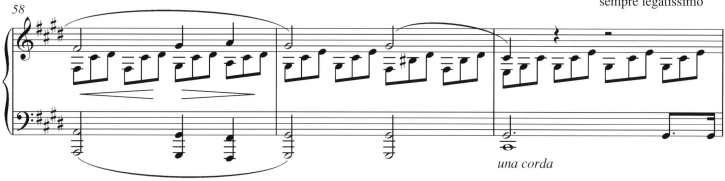

una corda

slentando

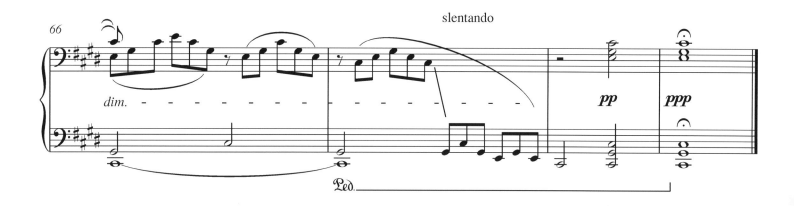

Sonata Pathétique, Op. 13
(2nd movement: Adagio cantabile)

Composed by Ludwig van Beethoven

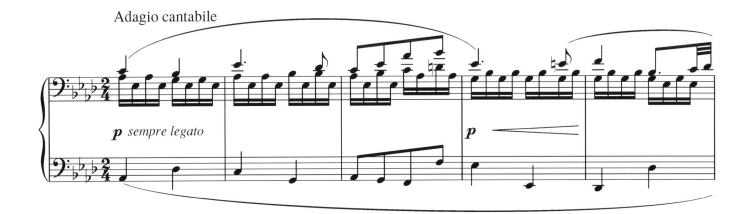

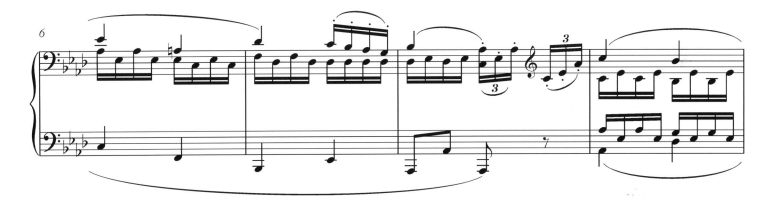

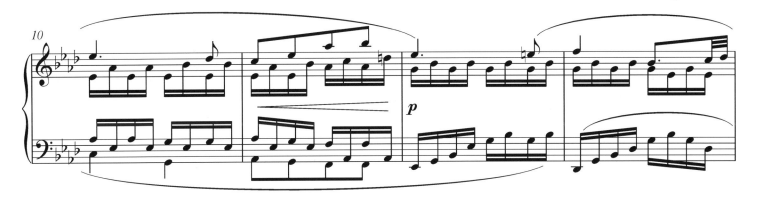

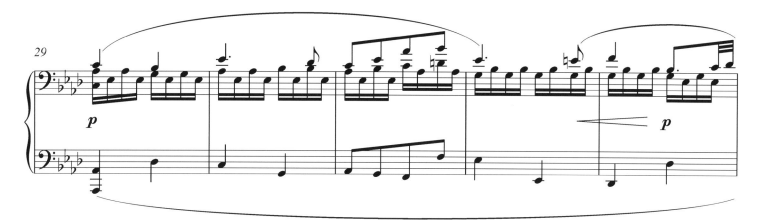

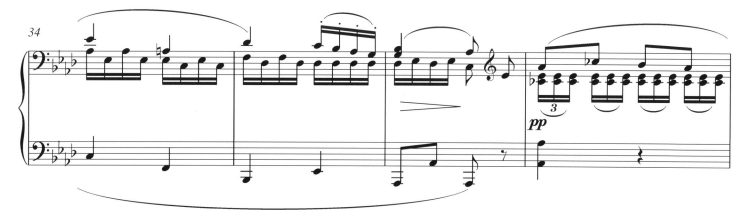

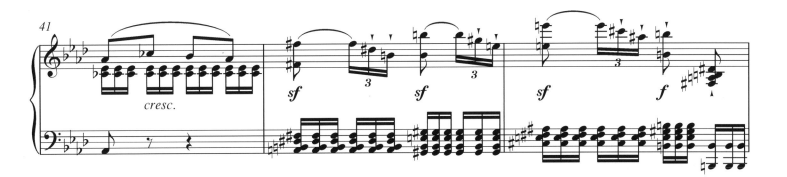

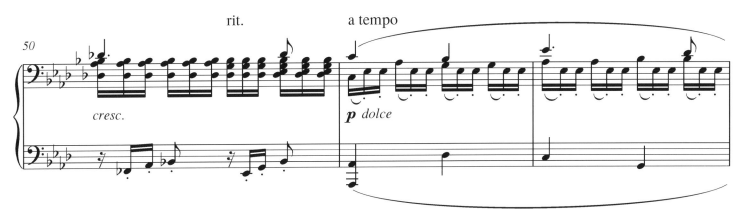

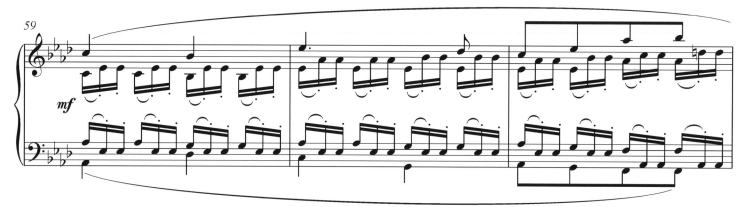

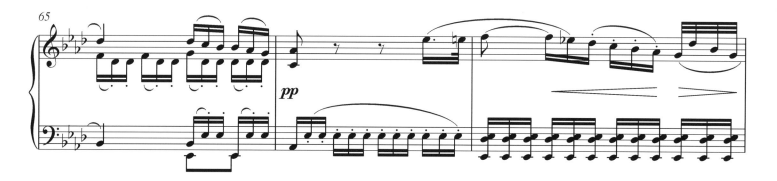

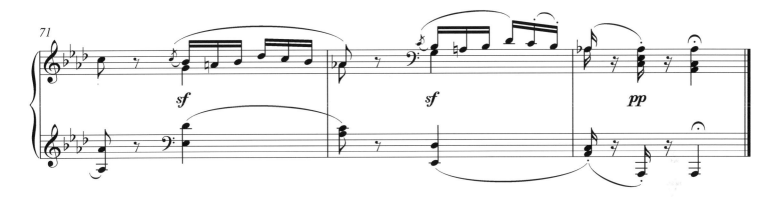

Bagatelle in G minor, Op. 119, No. 1

Composed by Ludwig van Beethoven

Allegretto

Rondo a Capriccio in G major, Op. 129
(Rage Over a Lost Penny)

Composed by Ludwig van Beethoven

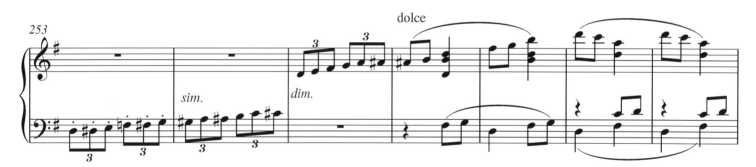

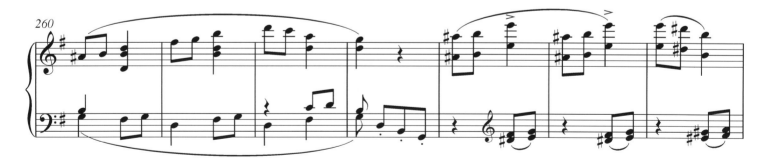

38

leggiermente

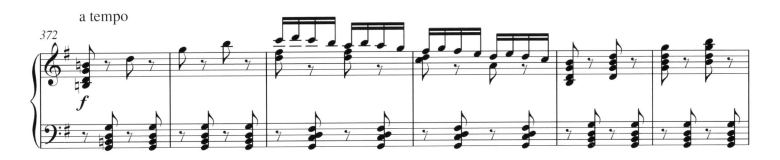

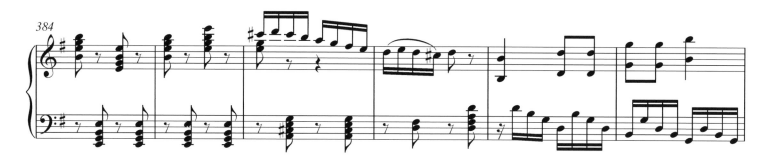

Sonata in D minor, Op. 31, No. 2

(1st movement)

Composed by Ludwig van Beethoven

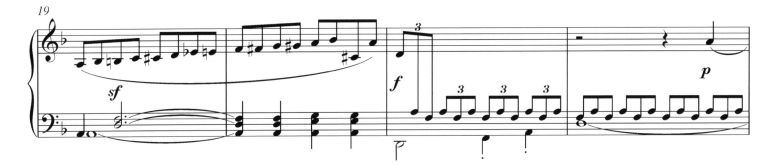

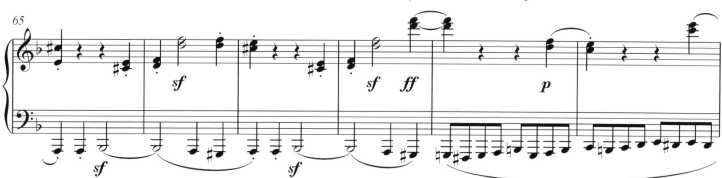

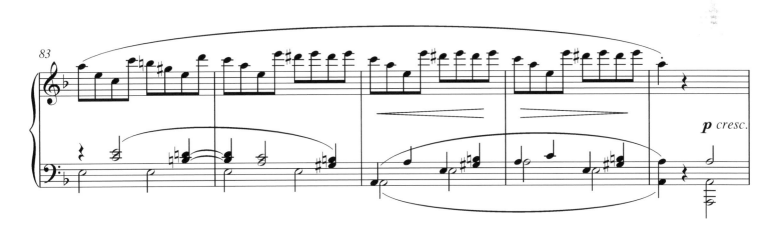

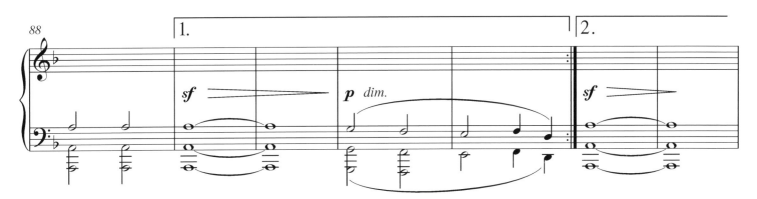

47

Largo

Allegro

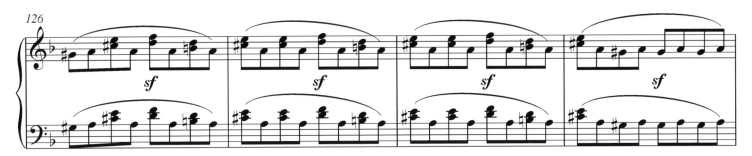

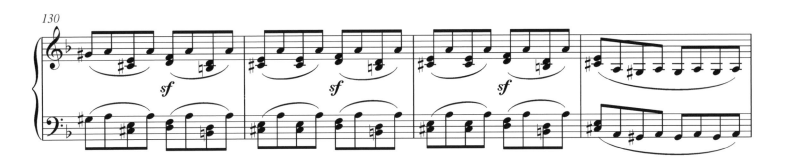

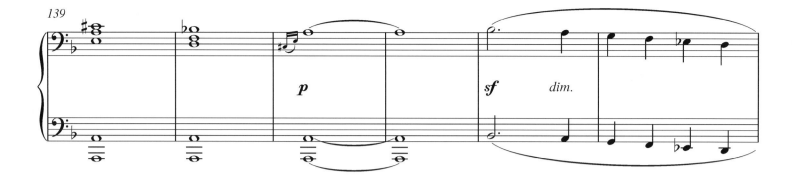

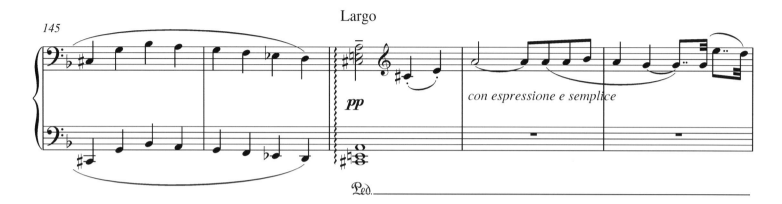

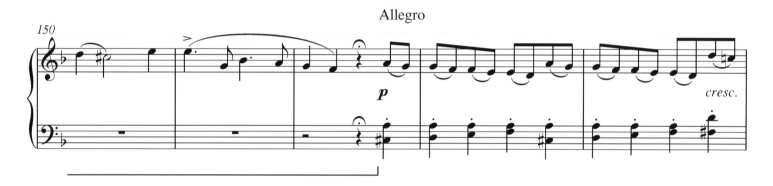

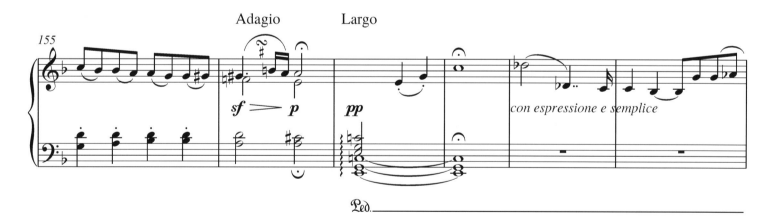

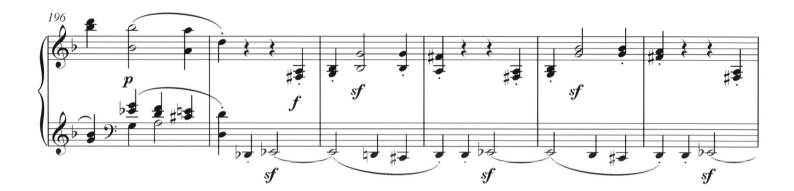

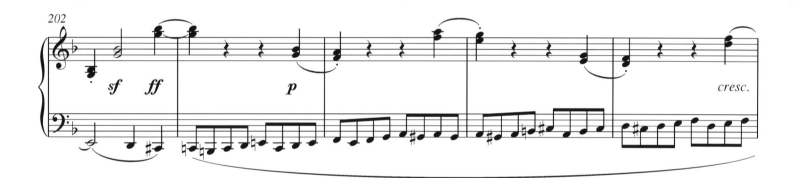

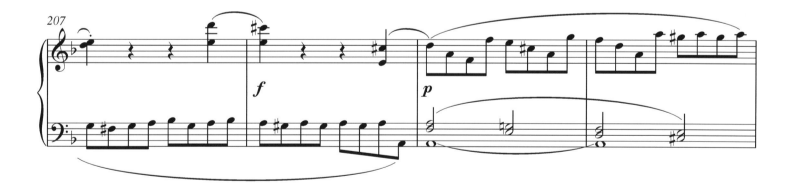

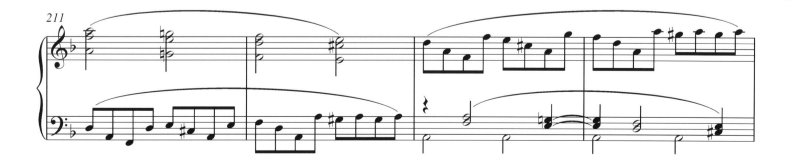

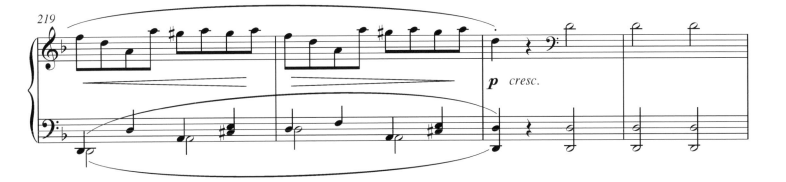

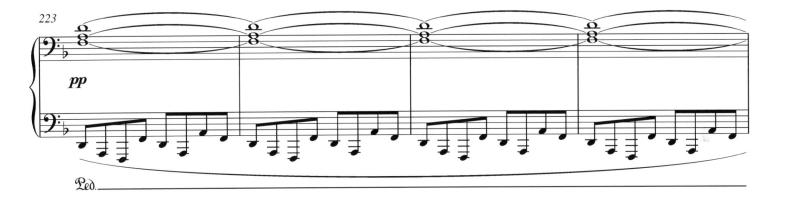

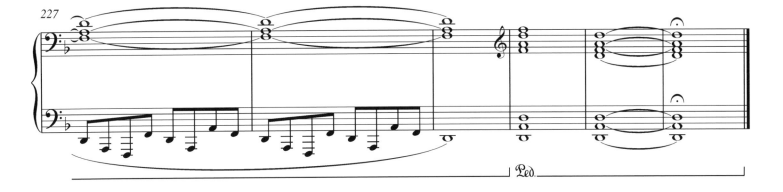

Sonata in G major, Op. 49, No. 2
(1st movement)

Composed by Ludwig van Beethoven

Allegro, ma non troppo

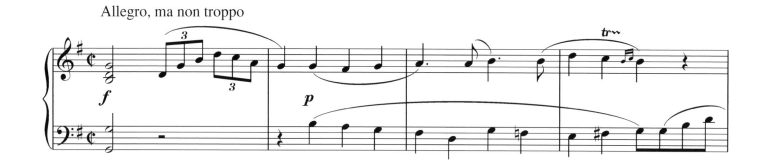

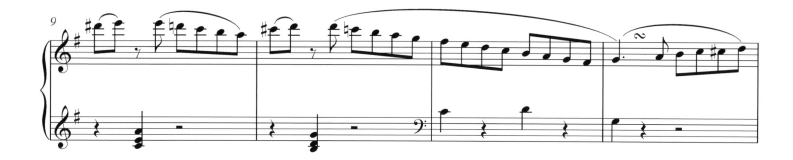

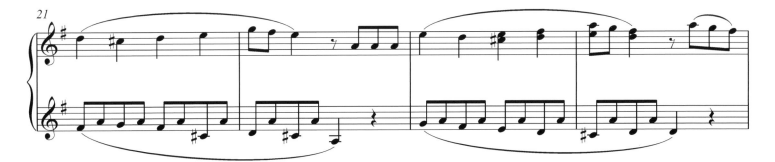

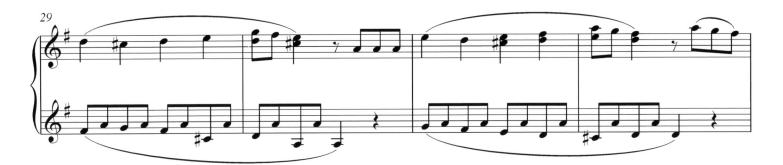

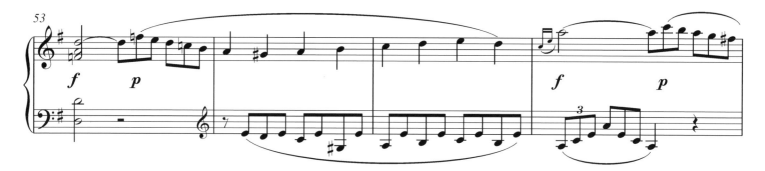

56

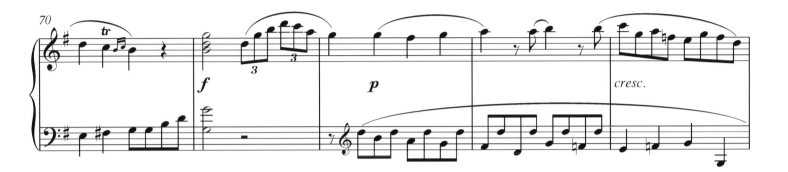

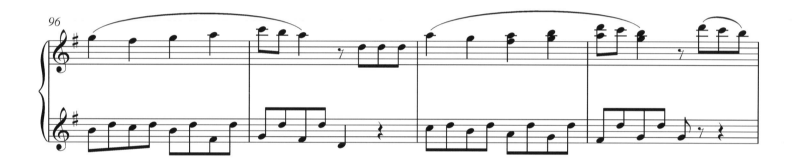

Sonata in G major, Op. 49, No. 2

(2nd movement)

Composed by Ludwig van Beethoven

Tempo di Menuetto

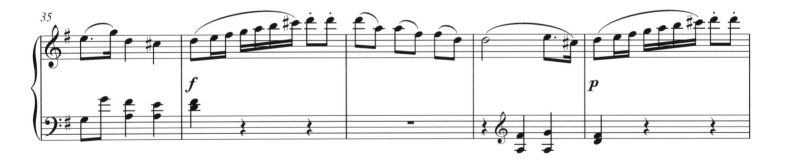

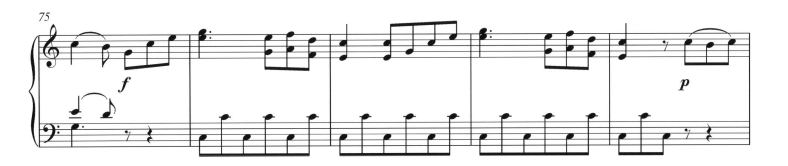

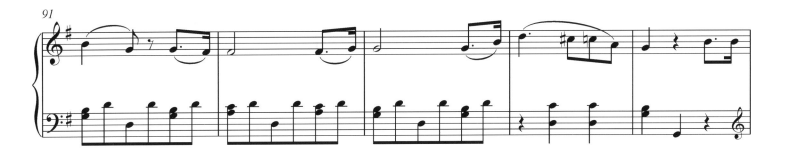

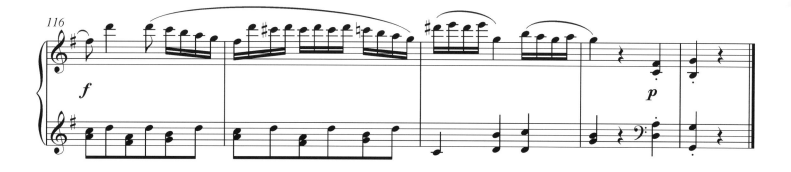

Sonata in G major, Op. 79
(2nd movement)

Composed by Ludwig van Beethoven

Vivace

Piano Concerto No.5 'Emperor', Op. 73

(2nd movement - Adagio un poco moto)

Composed by Ludwig van Beethoven

Adagio (♩ = 40)

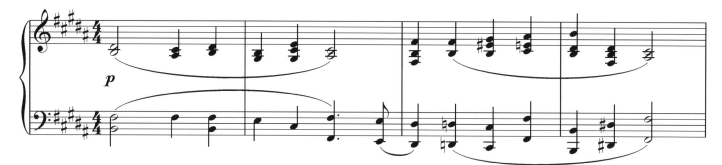

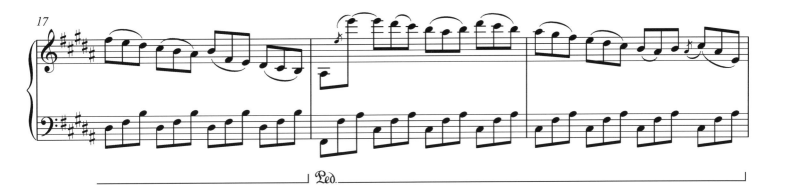

Symphony No. 3 'The Eroica', Op. 55

(1st movement theme)

Composed by Ludwig van Beethoven

Allegro con brio (♩. = 60)

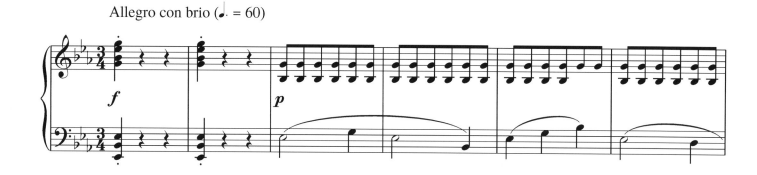

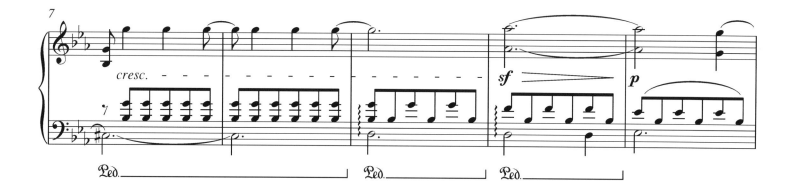

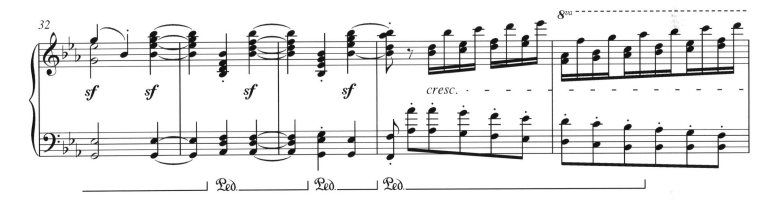

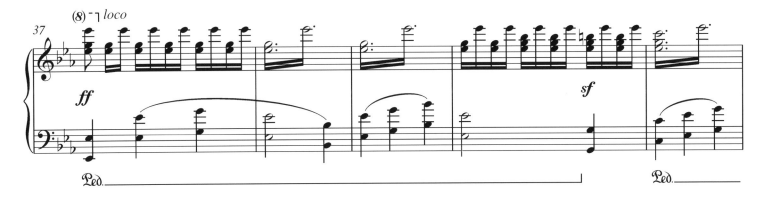

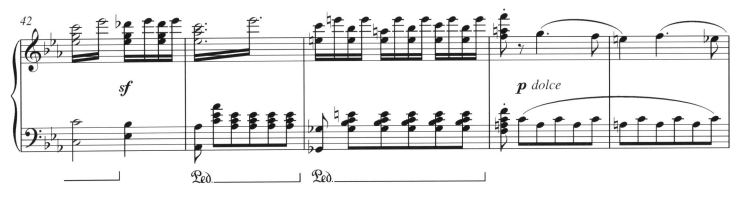

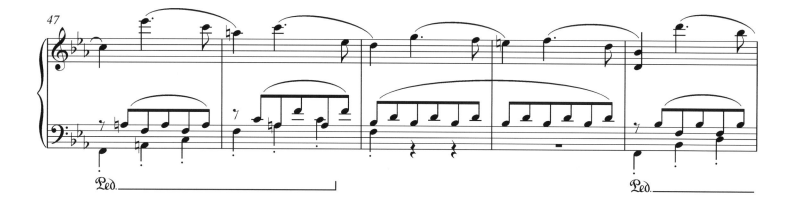

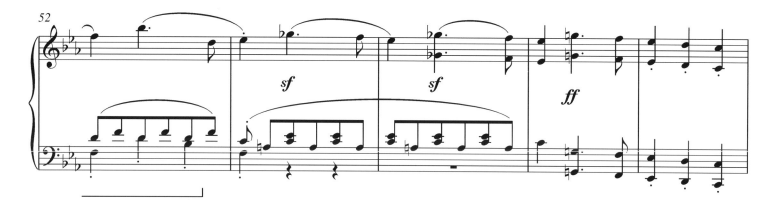

Symphony No. 5, Op. 67
(1st movement theme)

Composed by Ludwig van Beethoven

Allegro con brio (♩ = 108)

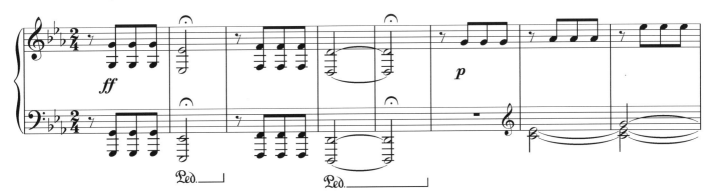

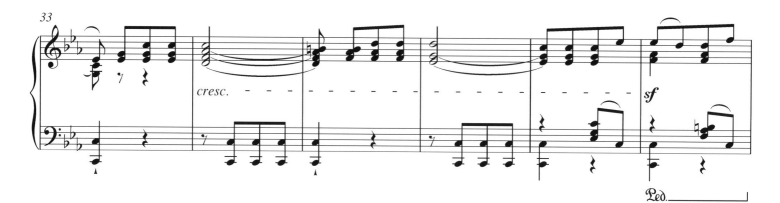

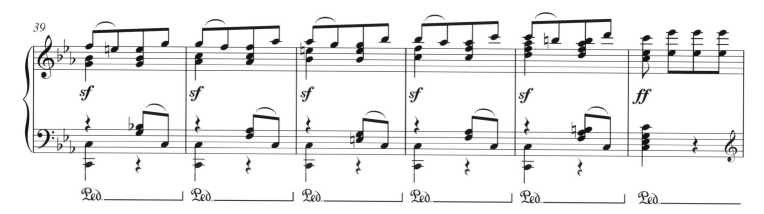

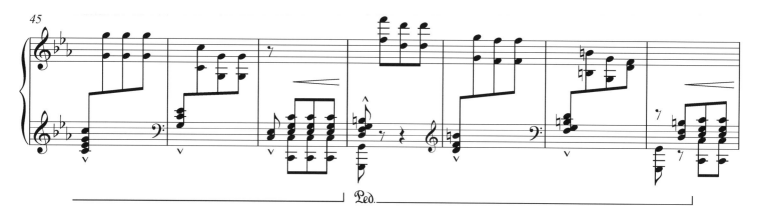

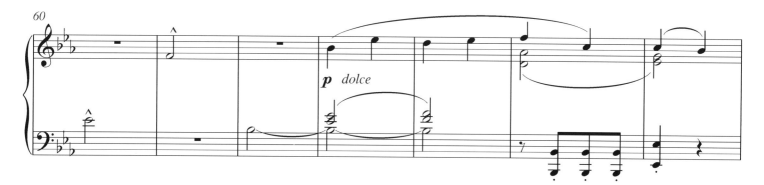

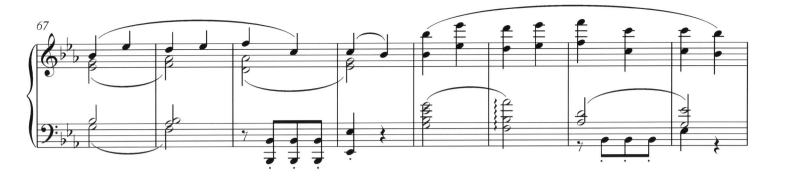

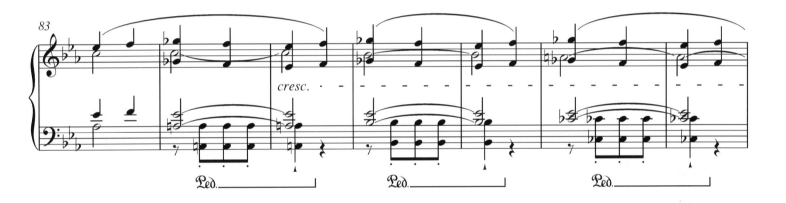

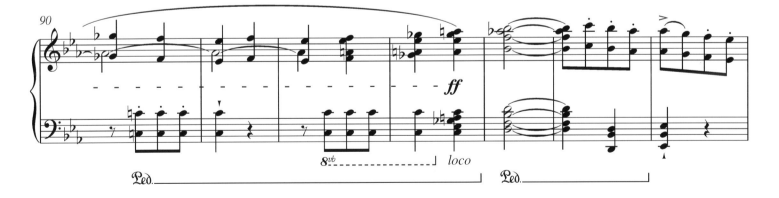

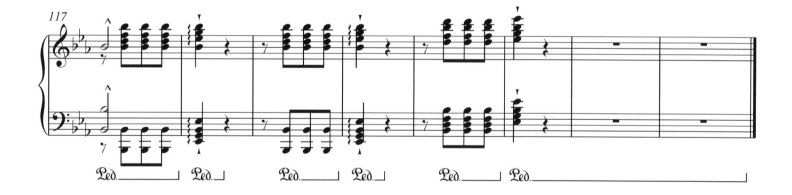

Symphony No. 6 'Pastoral', Op. 68
(Allegretto theme)

Composed by Ludwig van Beethoven

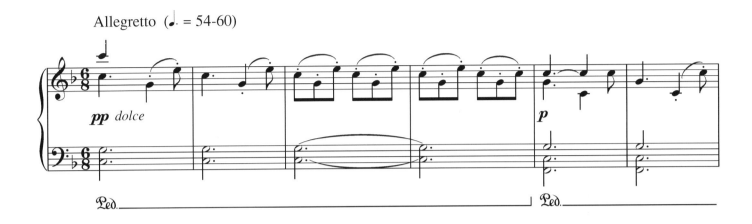

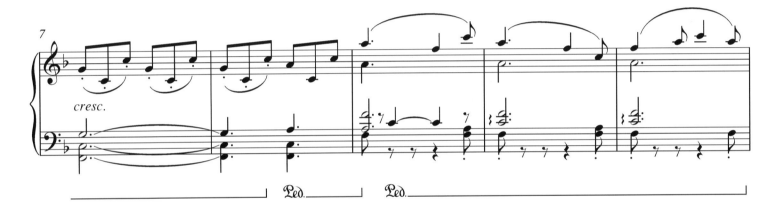

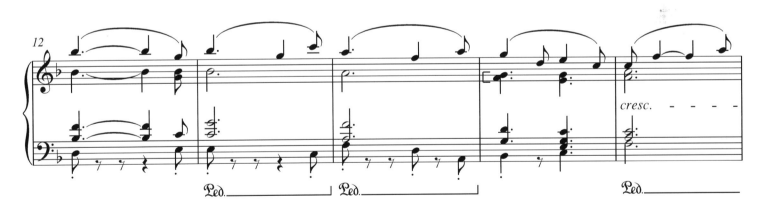

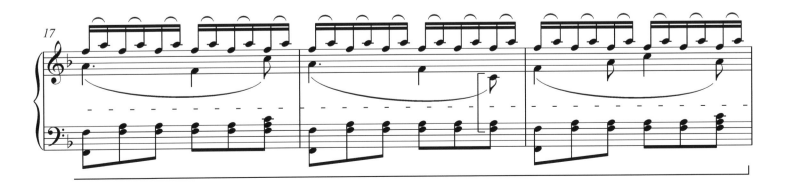

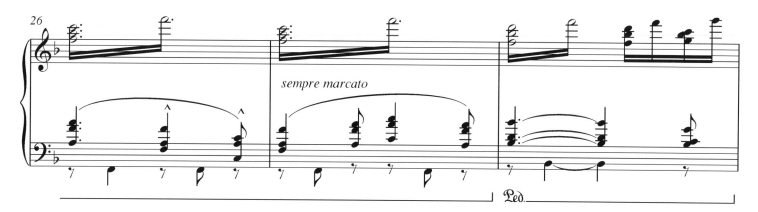

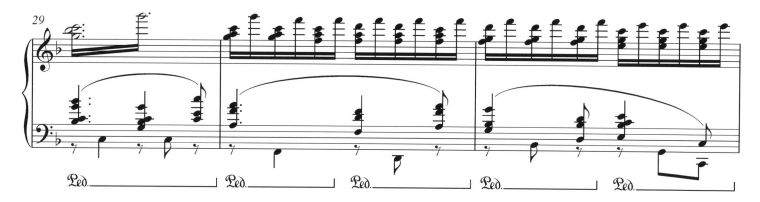

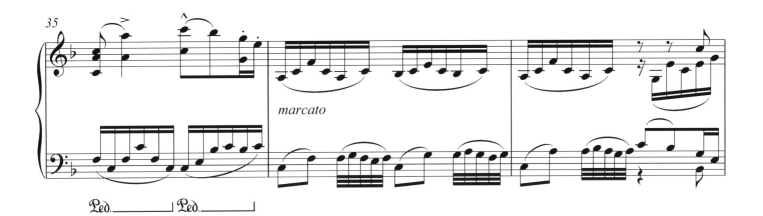

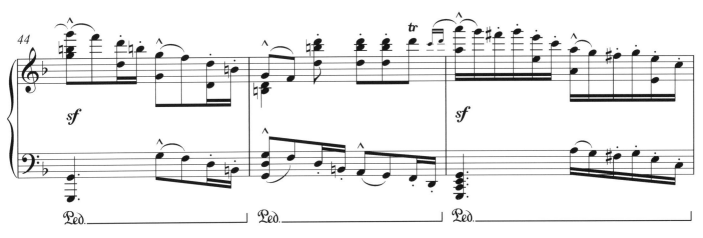

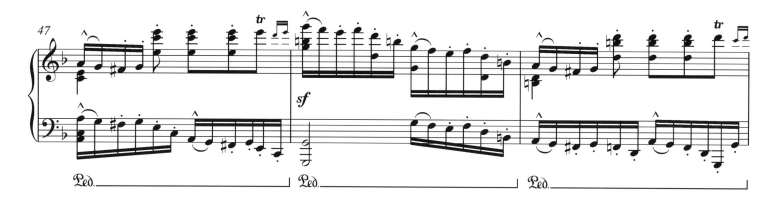

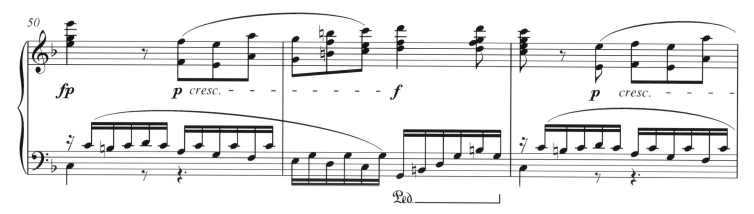

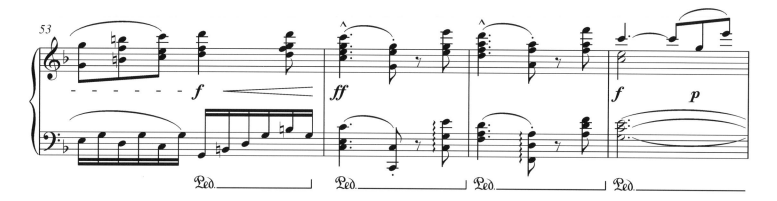

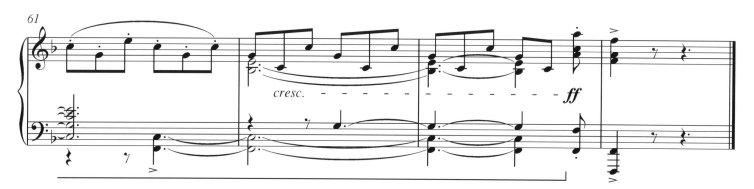

Symphony No. 7, Op. 92
(Allegretto theme)

Composed by Ludwig van Beethoven

Allegretto (♩ = 76)

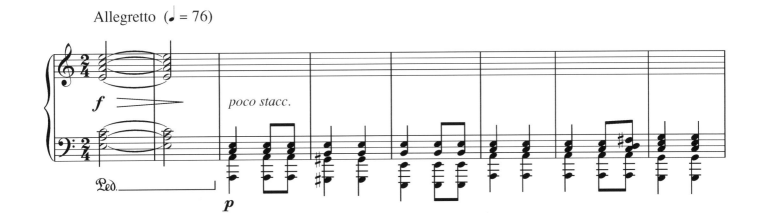

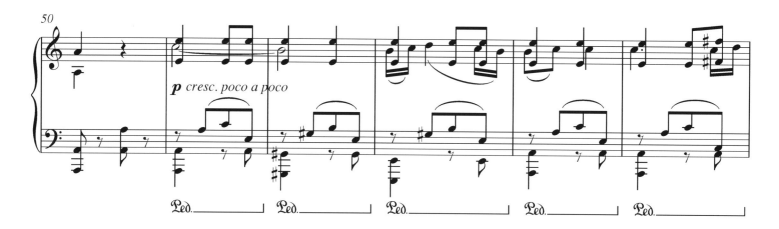

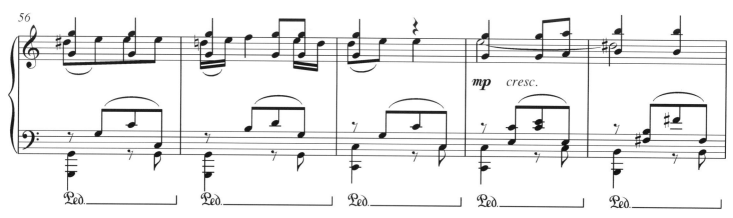

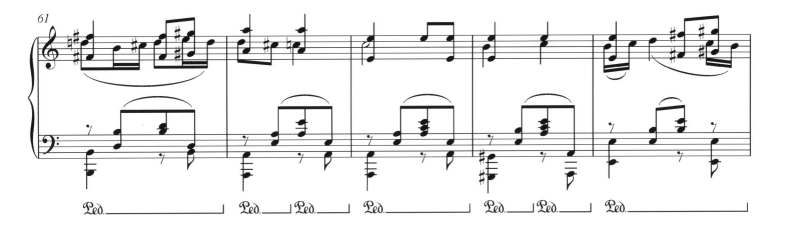

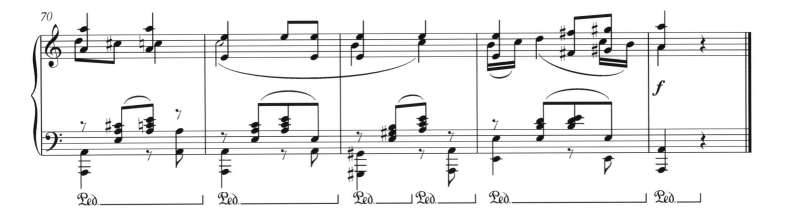

Symphony No. 9 'Choral', Op. 125

(Final movement 'Ode To Joy')

Composed by Ludwig van Beethoven

Allegro (♩ = 120)

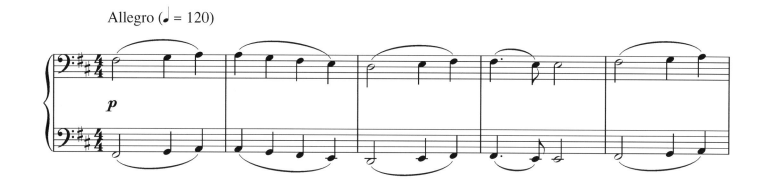

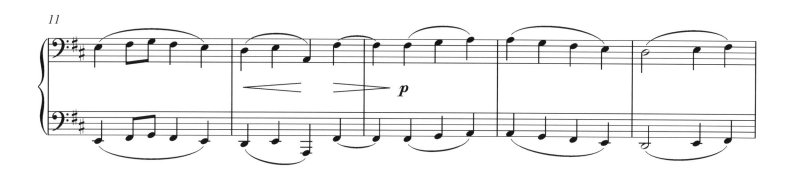

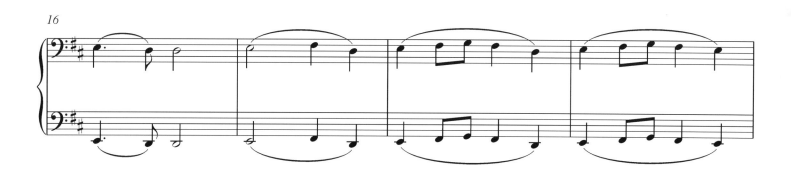

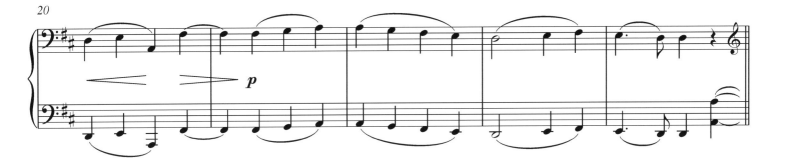

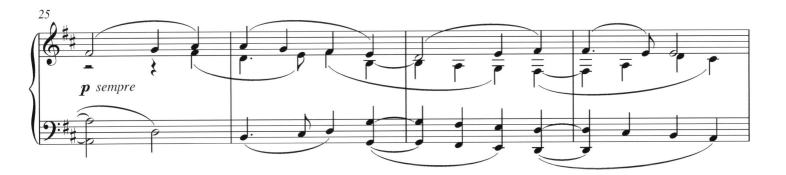

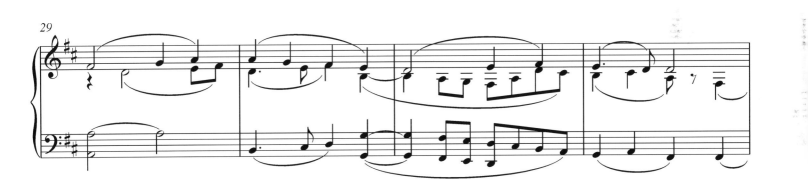

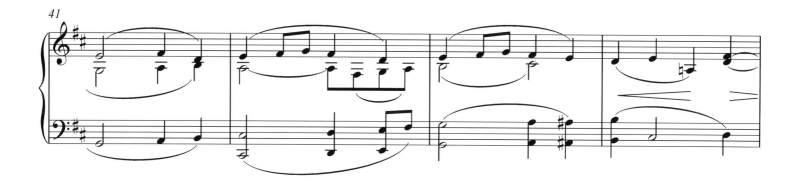

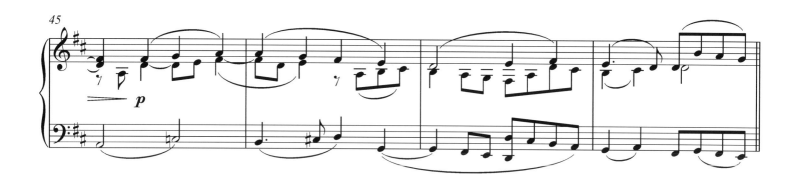

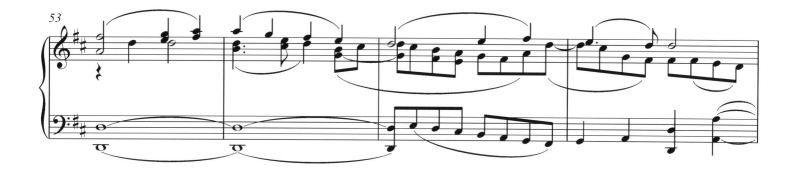

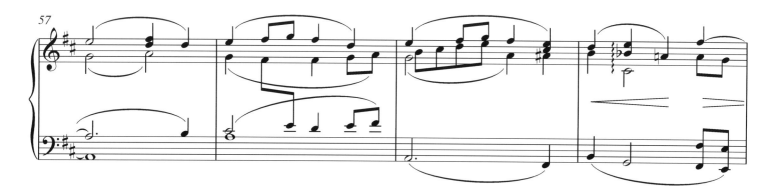

Violin Concerto Op. 61
(Rondo theme)

Composed by Ludwig van Beethoven

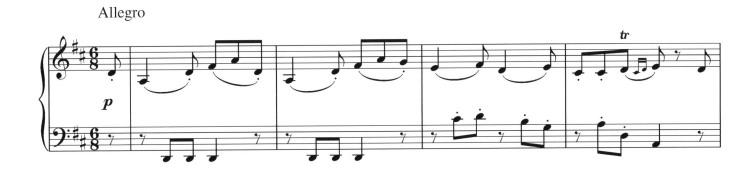

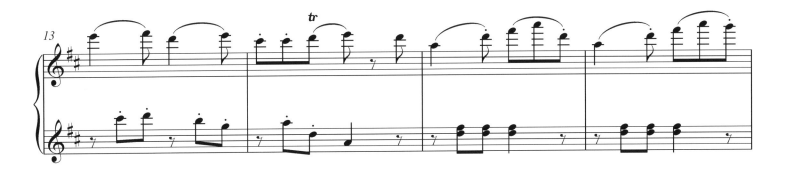

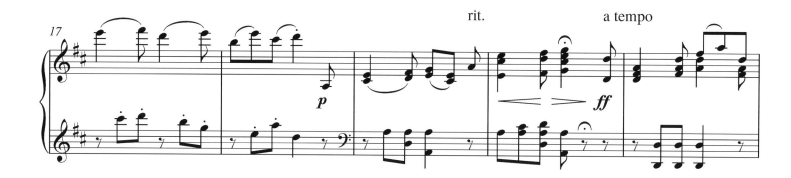

rit.　　　　　　　　　a tempo

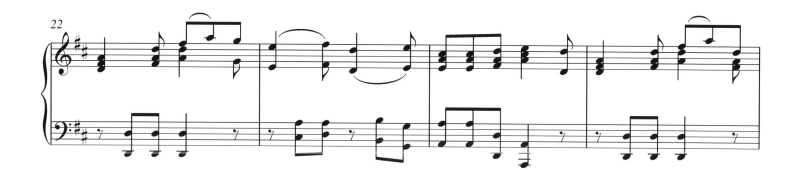

Bringing you the words and the music

All the latest music in print... rock & pop plus jazz, blues, country, classical and the best in West End show scores.

- Books to match your favourite CDs.

- Book-and-CD titles with high quality backing tracks for you to play along to. Now you can play guitar or piano with your favourite artist... or simply sing along!

- Audition songbooks with CD backing tracks for both male and female singers for all those with stars in their eyes.

- Can't read music? No problem, you can still play all the hits with our wide range of chord songbooks.

- Check out our range of instrumental tutorial titles, taking you from novice to expert in no time at all!

- Musical show scores include *The Phantom Of The Opera*, *Les Misérables*, *Mamma Mia* and many more hit productions.

- DVD master classes featuring the techniques of top artists.